D0910006

Wilner, Barry.

The composite guide to figure
skating

IN THIS SERIES

THE COMPOSITE GUIDE

to FIGURE SKATING

BARRY WILNER

CHELSEA HOUSE PUBLISHERS

Philadelphia

Produced by Choptank Syndicate, Inc. and Chestnut Productions

Senior Editor: Norman L. Macht
Editor and Picture Researcher: Mary E. Hull
Design and Production: Lisa Hochstein
Cover Illustrator: Cliff Spohn

Project Editor: Jim McAvoy
Art Direction: Sara Davis
Cover Design: Keith Trego

First Printing

1 3 5 7 9 8 6 4 2

Wilner, Barry.
     The composite guide to figure skating / by Barry Wilner.
          p.   cm.—(The composite guide)
     Includes bibliographical references and index.
     ISBN 0-7910-5864-6
     1. Skating—Juvenile literature. I. Title: Figure skating. II. Title. III. Series.
GV850.4. W57 2000

                                                          99-086454

CONTENTS

TARA AND MICHELLE

For almost a year, everyone knew it would come down to this: Michelle Kwan vs. Tara Lipinski for the 1998 Olympic gold medal. Their rivalry had existed for two-and-a-half years. Kwan, 17, and the American champion in 1996 and 1998, had also won the World Championship in '96. Lipinski, 15, had defeated Kwan for the 1997 U.S. and world titles.

The big showdown would be at the White Ring Arena in Nagano, Japan. First, however, came the Olympic pairs, men's, and dance competitions, all of them won by Russian skaters. No Americans won gold, silver, or bronze in those competitions. Not only were Kwan and Lipinski going after the most prized individual medal in women's sports, they were also trying to win at least one skating medal for the United States.

Kwan and Lipinski took very different routes to the Olympic Games. Kwan suffered a stress fracture to a toe on her left foot early in the season. She skipped many competitions, but at the National Championships in Philadelphia—which also served as the Olympic trials—she performed so magnificently that she earned 15 out of a possible 18 perfect marks of 6.0 for her artistry.

Riding such a high, Kwan went home to Lake Arrowhead, California, to train with her coach, Frank Carroll. She chose to skip the opening ceremony at Nagano and arrived nearly a week

Michelle Kwan, left, and Tara Lipinski, display the medals they won at the 1997 Worlds. Kwan and Lipinski proved to be stiff competition for one another at the 1998 winter Olympics held in Nagano, Japan.

into the Games. She stayed in a hotel with her family and Carroll, not in the athletes' village.

"I know how big a deal this is. I know how important this is to Michelle and everyone in the U.S. that she skates well," Carroll said.

"My job is to relieve as much tension in this kid as I can.

"What you do is what works for your athlete. If you want the best performance, you do what makes them comfortable, what makes them happy and what makes them well."

Lipinski, on the other hand, got to Nagano early, lived with the other athletes in dormitories, and attended the opening, plus hockey games and other skating events. She was having the time of her life.

"I wouldn't want to come to this like it was Worlds, or stay in a hotel or not come to opening ceremonies," she said. "This is so great. It's not like any other competition. I've been dreaming of it for so long. It's not like a world championship that you can go to every year. This is once in a lifetime."

Lipinski attended the first practice session available to her. She tried to meet hockey star Eric Lindros. She watched her friend Todd Eldredge when he practiced and competed.

But perhaps the most memorable moment for Lipinski before the women's skating began was meeting Akebono, a Japanese sumo wrestler.

"He's b-i-i-i-g," the 4' 10" 82-pound figure skater said with a shudder after meeting the 6' 8", 516-pound Akebono.

"She is small, very small," the Hawaiian-born Akebono said with a deep laugh. "Ahh, it's beauty and the beast."

It wasn't until five days after the opening ceremony that Kwan and Lipinski were on the ice together for practice. They pretty much ignored each other.

"We're not the best of friends," Kwan said, "but I think we have a friendly relationship." "We talked about jet lag while we were warming up," Lipinski said after practice.

"This is not like a bobsled, where they're all pushing the same sled," said Carroll. "You're out there by yourself."

Tara Lipinski reacts with relief and joy after successfully landing a difficult jump during her short program at the 1998 winter Olympics. Lipinski was in second place after the short program, trailing Michelle Kwan.

Tara Lipinski kisses her Olympic gold medal after winning the ladies' free skate long program at White Ring Arena on February 20, 1998, in Nagano, Japan. Michelle Kwan took the silver, and the bronze medal went to China's Lu Chen.

For the next week, they would attend the same practice sessions and work on their routines. Most days, they would meet with reporters, and both seemed relaxed and confident. Neither appeared to have an edge.

Kwan smoothly went through her workouts for her short program, worth one-third of the total score, performing to piano music by Rachmaninoff. Then she switched to her free skate, worth the other two-thirds, and skated to "Lyra Angelica." The foot injury didn't seem to bother her.

The pixieish Lipinski skated to music from the film *Anastasia*, in her short program. For the free skate, she skated to "The Rainbow," hoping she would soar that high. She rotated so quickly and so tightly when she jumped or spun that it was impossible for the untrained eye to know how many times she turned.

Lipinski was more of an athlete than Kwan, who was considered the most artistic female skater in the world. Usually, judges preferred the artist. But Kwan and Lipinski weren't thinking about that as they prepared for the short program.

"I enjoy being the Olympic favorite," Kwan said. "But you don't think about winning Olympic gold. My winning program is to skate well, and that's what I'm here to do."

Said Lipinski: "I feel very comfortable. I like being the underdog. It gives me a lot more things to think about and keeps me motivated."

Many others, including Nicole Bobek, the third American skater, were motivated for the world's biggest sports event. But none could come close to Kwan and Lipinski. It was strictly a two-woman show in the short program. Neither missed a beat in the 2-minute, 40-second routine, which has eight required elements. Kwan, thanks to a wonderful spiral—a gliding move with one blade on the ice as the other leg is extended in the air behind the body—placed first, Lipinski second.

"Before I started, I heard people cheering and I thought, 'I'm in heaven,'" Kwan said. "People clapping, billions of people watching on TV, and I'm skating. It's just me and the ice. When I'm on the ice, I don't think anybody can stop me."

Lipinski wasn't worried about being second after the short. She knew by winning the free skate (also called the long program), the gold would belong to her. She never doubted she could beat Kwan or anyone else.

"There was nothing more I could do," she said. "I couldn't ask for anything better. It gave me a lot of confidence going into the long program."

It had come down to this: the winner of the free skate two nights later would be the Olympic champion. Both skaters had strong workouts in brief practice sessions between the short and long programs. Nerves weren't getting to them. The attention wasn't bothering them; Lipinski, in particular, seemed to rejoice in it. They were ready.

Kwan had drawn the first spot in the final group, where the top six finishers from the short program were placed. Lipinski was next-to-last. When that last group of skaters came onto the ice at White Ring Arena to warm up, the crowd cheered loudly and cameras clicked everywhere. American flags and banners waved throughout the grandstands.

But when Kwan took the ice to begin her program, the arena fell silent. Not until she majestically landed her first combination—a triple Lutz-double toe loop—did the fans erupt in cheers. Smoothly, but without much emotion or expression, Kwan completed her routine. It was very good but not nearly on the level of her near-perfect performance at the Nationals.

"It seemed like I was in my own world," Kwan said. "I didn't open up and let myself go." The judges' marks placed Kwan first across the board but with plenty of room to move Lipinski to the top. First, though, Lipinski had to do her part. Tara was like a whirlwind on the ice. Every jump was quick and precise, including a triple loop-triple loop combination that no one else even attempted at the Olympics. She spun like a top but always in control. Her smile grew wider and wider with every move, every minute.

When she finished the last spin, Lipinski literally ran to center ice, giggling and waving and bowing. There were hugs for coach Richard Callaghan—and anyone else in the area—as she walked off and awaited her marks.

Six judges scored Lipinski first, while three favored Kwan, including the American judge. When those marks told her she was the youngest Olympic figure skating champion ever, beating Sonja Henie, the first great female skater, Lipinski leapt out of her seat and danced a jig of pure joy.

"There is nothing that could be better for me," she said breathlessly. "Anything that goes on in the future, I will be so content with what I have done. I also think whcn I stepped on the ice, I had a feeling I knew what the Olympics were about. I had that feeling of just pure joy, and I went out there and put it in my program. It felt so great, I can't even explain it. Knowing against all odds under all that pressure, you did it. I will always remember it."

She and Kwan will always be remembered for their spectacular showdown and their rousing rivalry, which pretty much ended at Nagano. Lipinski soon turned professional, while Kwan remained eligible for the 2002 Olympics in Salt Lake City.

If they meet again when both are pros, it won't be the same. It wouldn't be fair to expect anything like what they achieved in Nagano. For two nights, in the most stressful of circumstances, Tara Lipinski and Michelle Kwan performed like champions. No one can ask for more than that.

HISTORY OF THE SPORT

2

As far back as the late 15th century, people were using wooden skates to cross frozen ponds. It was a matter of transportation. But those same people soon found a way to entertain themselves by racing each other, then by tracing figures on the ice. When the skates began being made of metal in the 16th century, two sports were born: speed skating and figure skating.

The first known skating club was organized in Edinburgh, Scotland, in the late 1700s. In 1772, Robert Jones of England wrote the first book on ice skating. In those early days, the figure skating competitions were judged on the quality of the tracings, not on the style the skater used. They were local events, and Britain was the center of the figure skating world by the early 19th century.

Although the sport attracted mostly the wealthy in the 1800s, skates themselves were not expensive; they could be bought for as little as one dollar in the 1850s.

By then, the first skating club in the United States had been organized but not just for play. Members of the Philadelphia Skating Club and Humane Society also skated onto the frozen Schuykill River to rescue people who fell through the ice.

Figure skating's popularity really took off in New York in the 1860s when a rink was opened on a pond in Central Park. Legend has it that on

Norway's Sonja Henie was the original superstar of women's figure skating—winning back-to-back Olympic gold medals in 1928, 1932, and 1936. The first skater to incorporate ballet and popular dance moves, Henie also set a lasting trend with her short, flashy skating outfits.

Christmas Day in 1860, 100,000 people came to the park to skate. In 1863, the first national championships were held in Troy, New York. One reason the sport grew so quickly in America was that women were welcomed equally with men. That was true in almost no other sport at that time.

The father of modern figure skating was an American, Jackson Haines, who brought music and dance steps to the sport. Few people involved in U.S. skating accepted Haines's style, so he left America to live in Europe. While there, he toured in shows that allowed him to present his brand of skating, and he was wildly popular. Thanks to Haines, figure skating became entertainment as well as a means of exercise.

London's Glaciarium, opened in 1876, was the first rink with man-made ice. Soon, many such indoor rinks were being built. But the sport needed some direction, so the International Skating Union (ISU) was formed in 1892. Four years later, the ISU held the first World Championships, at which the figure-eight tracings were the main competition.

Through the decades, various skating pioneers such as Jones and Haines have contributed to the development of the sport. Such jumps as the Axel, Lutz, and Salchow are named after the men who first did them.

Axel Paulsen of Norway developed a jump with a front takeoff. It is still the only one done in that manner, and it is the most difficult jump because a skater makes an extra half turn before landing. To have a chance to win a medal at the highest level today, male skaters must have at least one triple Axel in their program.

Sweden's Ulrich Salchow, who won 10 World Championships in the early 1900s, invented a jump with a takeoff from the back inside edge of one foot and a backward landing on the outside edge of the opposite foot.

Alois Lutz came up with a jump in which the skater digs the toe pick of one skate into the ice and takes off backward after a long approach. The skater enters the jump skating in one direction and finishes skating in the opposite direction.

An 1887 illustration from Harper's Weekly *depicts an elegant skating party on a pond in New York's Central Park. The first skating rink opened in Central Park in 1860, when as many as 100,000 people came out to skate on Christmas Day.*

Approved as an Olympic sport in 1896, figure skating made its Olympic debut in 1908 in an indoor rink at the summer Games, because there were no winter Games until 1924. Ulrich Salchow won the men's event, and Madge Syers of England, skating at her home rink in London, was the women's champion. She also won the bronze in pairs that year with her husband.

It wasn't until 1920 that figure skating returned to the Olympics, again in the summer at Antwerp, Belgium. It was left out of the 1912 and 1916 Games because the sport was part of the Nordic Games, which were a smaller version of what would become the winter Olympics and also because many people on the International Olympic Committee (IOC) considered skaters and skiers to be professionals. At the time, the Olympics were just for amateurs who did not earn a living from their sports.

Peggy Fleming performs during the freestyle skate at the 1968 winter Olympics in Grenoble, France. Fleming, the only member of the U.S. team to win a gold medal at the 1968 winter Olympics, brought renewed interest to the sport.

By 1924, when the first winter Olympics were held in Chamonix, France, the World and U.S. Championships were going strong. But the early success stories in skating were scored by the Europeans. Not until after World War II did a non-European win a world title. Since then, the Americans and Canadians have been as strong as any other nation's skaters.

The first superstar of figure skating was Sonja Henie of Norway. From Henie in the 1920s to Tara Lipinski and Michelle Kwan in the late 1990s, women have been the headliners of the sport. But there have been some great male performers, from Gillis Grafstrom and Karl Shafer in the early years, to Dick Button, Scott Hamilton, and Brian Boitano later on.

In Henie's day, looks, grace, and speed on the ice mattered most. Jumps weren't important. That remained true into the late 1960s, when the tracings in compulsory figures counted for much more of the score than the free skate, which included the jumps, spins, and footwork we are now used to seeing.

When Peggy Fleming's 1968 Olympic performance sparked a rapid growth of spectator interest, television took notice. ISU officials realized the programs needed more action. So the free skate grew in importance until it accounted for two-thirds of the total score for singles and pairs. The compulsories were dropped in 1991, gone for all but ice dancing, where they are worth 20 percent.

Singles and pairs now have a technical (or short) program, which is worth two-thirds of the total score and has eight required elements. Ice dancing has an original dance (30 percent) and free dance (50 percent) to go with compulsory dances.

In 1994 the ISU and IOC allowed professionals who had lost their Olympic eligibility to return for the Lillehammer Games. It was a one time opportunity.

Today, there are separate events run by the ISU for Olympic-eligible skaters and professional competitions for those who are not eligible for the Olympics. There are even some combined professional/amateur events in which both groups can compete.

Television networks have created their own competitions and shows. Many of the great skaters of the 1980s and 1990s appear on tours such as Stars on Ice, created by Scott Hamilton, and Champions on Ice, created by Tom Collins. But on a winter's day, the purest form of figure skating still can be found down at the frozen ponds where it all began.

THE ICE QUEENS

Figure skating is a woman's sport like no other. While women athletes have had their moments of fame in other sports, only in figure skating are the women almost always the top attraction. They must be charming and glamorous. At the same time, they must be athletic and tireless.

SONJA HENIE

Often called the creator of modern figure skating, Sonja Henie won more World Championships and Olympic gold medals than any singles performer. She also took the sport from the frozen ponds of Europe to the silver screen in Hollywood.

Henie sometimes is compared to Babe Ruth, Red Grange, and Arnold Palmer, men who made baseball, football, and golf popular throughout America. In some ways, her influence was even stronger, because, before Henie, her sport barely had a following in most countries. After Henie, women's figure skating became the featured act of the winter Olympics.

Henie began skating when she was five years old. By the age of nine, she was the national champion of Norway. At the tender age of 11, Henie skated in the 1924 Olympics in Chamonix, France. At 14, she won her first World Championship. Today, 14-year-olds usually are competing in the novice or junior levels, one step below the top competition.

Gold medal winner Katarina Witt, known for being an actress as well as an athlete, mimics Michael Jackson's moonwalk at the closing ceremony of the 1988 winter Olympics in Calgary.

At the 1928 Olympics in St. Moritz, Switzerland, Henie became known as the Ice Princess. Just 15, she easily won the gold medal, combining the smooth dance she had learned as a ballet student with unmatched energy. She was the biggest star of the Games.

But Henie wanted more than medals. She wanted to make the sport her own. As a competitor, she did that by winning every World Championship from 1927 to the time she turned professional in 1936 and by winning the 1932 and 1936 Olympic crowns.

But Henie did much more. She set a new fashion style with her short skirts and flashy costumes. She moved so quickly around the rink it made her look like a speed skater in comparison to the other competitors. Her dance skills easily got the crowds involved. Suddenly, figure skating no longer belonged to the rich. It was a sport that interested everyone.

Still, Henie wanted more. In 1936, with nothing left to conquer as a competitor, she signed a contract to make movies for Twentieth Century-Fox. Darryl F. Zanuck, one of the most powerful and famous men in Hollywood, believed he could make Henie as popular as child star Shirley Temple. Henie's first of 12 films, *One in a Million*, was an instant hit. Zanuck was right: only Temple's films earned more than Henie's.

Henie also began touring in a show that became nearly as popular as her films. She sparked a boom in ice rink production in the United States as thousands of young girls were inspired to become figure skaters.

After she retired from skating, Henie became an art collector. She died of leukemia in 1969, a wealthy woman who had changed her sport. Henie was inducted into the Figure Skating Hall of Fame in 1976.

MADGE SYERS

Before Madge Syers of England came along, the World Championships were reserved for men. Her husband, Edgar, was a top men's competitor. But Madge Syers challenged the system by filing an entry for the 1902 Worlds. Because there were no rules preventing her from competing, she was allowed to skate, and she beat all but one man.

Her success embarrassed the ISU, which banned women from competing against men at Worlds. The ISU did not set up a women's World Championship until 1906, and Syers won it the first two years.

Meanwhile, Madge won the British Championships in 1903 and 1904, when she defeated her husband.

When figure skating first became part of the Olympics in 1908, it was held at Syers's home rink in London. She won the gold and took a bronze in pairs with Edgar. Syers is the only woman to win two figure skating medals at one Olympics.

Syers was only 36 when she died from complications in childbirth. In 1981, she was posthumously inducted into the Figure Skating Hall of Fame.

BARBARA ANN SCOTT

The focus in women's skating shifted to North America after World War II, and Canada's Barbara Ann Scott became the first great champion from the Western Hemisphere. She won the 1947 and '48 Worlds and earned the gold medal at the 1948 Olympics.

Scott survived a dispute over a gift she was given by the mayor of her hometown of Ottawa. The mayor gave her a car, and members of the IOC questioned if it was considered a payment, which would have cost Scott her amateur standing and Olympic eligibility. When the mayor took back the car (he returned it to Scott after the Olympics) she was allowed to compete.

Scott made it into the Hall of Fame in 1979.

TENLEY ALBRIGHT

In 1956 Tenley Albright became the first U.S. skater to win the Olympic gold medal. The first American woman world champion (1953), Albright won five straight national titles.

When she was 11 years old, Albright was stricken with polio, a disease which often killed youngsters in those days. But she recovered quickly and used skating as a way of getting in shape and staying healthy. Before long, Albright won the U.S. junior Championships.

She successfully defended her U.S. senior title in 1954 and '55 and also won her second World crown even though she was attending Radcliffe College full-time as a medical student. Albright then attended Harvard Medical School and became a surgeon.

In 1976, Dr. Tenley Albright was inducted into the Hall of Fame.

CAROL HEISS

Just as Albright's career reached the top, another American skater came along to challenge her.

Sixteen-year-old Carol Heiss, left, and 21-year-old Tenley Albright skate together while warming up for the 1956 U.S. Figure Skating Championship.

Carol Heiss would become the only U.S. woman to win five Worlds. As she was rising in the skating ranks, Heiss and Albright had a thrilling rivalry, even though Heiss was several years younger.

It wasn't until the 1956 Worlds, after Heiss had won the silver behind Albright at the Olympics in Cortina, Italy, that the order of finish reversed. Finally, Heiss beat Albright.

Heiss was the first skater to benefit from television coverage at the Olympics. The 1960 Games were held in Squaw Valley, California, and Heiss was selected to recite the Olympic oath, the first woman to do so. Then her beautiful moves, smooth spins, and grace on the ice captured the imagination of America as she won the gold medal.

Heiss later married fellow Olympic figure skating champion Hayes Jenkins and left the sport for 18 years. She returned to become a top coach and was honored with a Hall of Fame spot in 1976.

PEGGY FLEMING

Women's figure skating was popular before Peggy Fleming, but thanks to her elegance, the sport reached new levels. Fleming joined forces with Carlo Fassi, perhaps the best of all coaches, who helped her overcome her shyness and develop her skills.

Fleming already owned five U.S. titles and two of her three World crowns when she came to Grenoble, France, for the 1968 winter Olympics.

An expert in the compulsory figure-eights, Fleming was so far ahead after performing them that she had nearly clinched the gold medal. ABC televised the free skate live via satellite, a first for the Olympics. The announcers made sure everyone knew Fleming's dress was sewn by her mother and that this budding star had once been too shy to speak.

Fleming's majestic performance made her one of the most popular sports figures in the world. It also boosted figure skating to a new height; even men began watching the ice queens.

Fleming retired from competition after winning the 1968 Worlds and began touring with Ice Follies. Since 1981, five years after she made the Hall of Fame, she has been a figure skating commentator for ABC. In 1998, Peggy Fleming won her toughest battle, with breast cancer. She has since become a spokeswoman for breast cancer awareness, and she has written her autobiography.

JANET LYNN

Although she ruled American skating from 1969 to 1973, Janet Lynn didn't reach the level of Albright, Heiss, or Fleming. But she did gain as much popularity.

Nobody was as imaginative or daring a free skater as Lynn. Unlike Fleming, she struggled with compulsories, which meant Lynn had little chance of winning international events. But she was a force in the free skate.

Even when she was on the junior level, Lynn was performing triple jumps that many seniors didn't attempt. She was so skillful that even if she made a major mistake in a free skate program, Lynn could win that portion of the competition, if not the overall championship.

After finishing third at the 1972 Olympics—without compulsories, she would have won handily—Lynn signed the richest deal ever for a female athlete, $1.45 million to join Ice Follies. She skated for two years in the show before asthma forced her retirement. She was inducted into the Hall of Fame in 1994.

DOROTHY HAMILL

Carlo Fassi coached another great champion, Hall of Fame member Dorothy Hamill. Unlike Fleming, Hamill was anything but a sure thing coming to the 1976 Innsbruck, Austria, winter Olympics.

Hamill was best known for her distinctive short wedge hairstyle, which *Life* magazine once called one of the most important fashion statements in 50 years, and for her camel spin: the Hamill Camel. She was the most precise and smoothest spinner in the world, but in the days when jumping was becoming more of a key element for women, Hamill worried that spins might not be enough to win on the sport's biggest stage.

Hamill skated so well in the compulsories and the short program (which had been instituted after the 1972 season) that she needed to be merely ordinary in the free skate. She was anything but ordinary. Before a worldwide television audience, she outskated the flashier Europeans, displaying an unbeatable charm

Dorothy Hamill spins her way to a gold medal during the free skating program at the 1976 winter Olympics in Innsbruck, Austria.

that carried over to the "kiss and cry" area, where skaters sit to watch their scores posted. Hamill did not wear her glasses when she skated, so she squinted deeply as coach Fassi read off her marks, which made her the gold medal winner.

Before long, young girls everywhere were wearing the Hamill haircut, and she landed a contract with Clairol. Hamill also skated professionally and appeared in television specials into the late '90s.

KATARINA WITT

The only woman to win more than one Olympic title since Sonja Henie, Katarina Witt was the first great singles skater from a Communist country. Witt grew up in East Germany, where youngsters were placed in athletic programs to develop their skills. She was five when she began skating and nine when she was assigned to Jutta Mueller, the top coach in the nation.

Although Mueller controlled nearly every area of Witt's life, the skater accepted the system because she knew it could lead her to the top. And it did, as she won six European Championships, four Worlds, and the Olympic gold medal in 1984 and 1988.

Considered as much an actress as an athlete, Witt was known for her ability to perform as a character. She wasn't the best jumper, nor the best spinner. But she was so expressive and technically strong that her weaknesses rarely mattered.

After upsetting American skater Rosalynn Sumners at the 1984 Sarajevo Games, Witt became a mystery, appearing outside East

Kristi Yamaguchi, shown during her free skating program at the 1992 winter Olympics in Albertville, France, won a gold medal for her performance.

Germany only for major competitions. When she came to America, she was rarely allowed to meet the media or fans.

In 1988, Witt and American challenger Debi Thomas both skated to music from the opera *Carmen*, so their meeting at the Calgary Olympics was known as "Dueling Carmens." Witt easily won her second gold. She then wowed the audience at the exhibition following the Games by doing Michael Jackson's moonwalk, showing a new part of her on-ice personality.

After that performance, there was no stopping Witt. She toured in professional shows and made movies and television appearances. She returned to the Olympics in 1994, when pros were allowed back for the Lillehammer Games, and skated a tribute to the people of war-torn Sarajevo, where she had won her first Olympic gold medal in 1984.

Witt, a Hall of Famer since 1995, twice made *People* magazine's list of the most beautiful people in the world.

KRISTI YAMAGUCHI

For much of her early career, Kristi Yamaguchi was a winner in pairs skating; she and partner Rudy Galindo won two national titles and were strong competitors in Worlds. But after a disappointing 1990 Worlds in both singles and pairs, she decided to skate solo only, and her career took off.

Not the greatest jumper, Yamaguchi was certainly an elegant skater. Her spins were tight and fast, her spirals and footwork unmatched. Heading to the 1992 Albertville Games, Yamaguchi was ranked the number one figure skater in the world, and her countrywomen Tonya Harding and Nancy Kerrigan were second and third. There was talk of a U.S. sweep.

They came close, led by Yamaguchi, who, just two years after dropping pairs, became the Olympic gold medalist in singles. Nancy Kerrigan placed third and Tonya Harding, fourth.

Surprisingly, with the next Olympics just two years away—the IOC changed the schedule so the winter Games would not be in the same year as the summer Games—Yamaguchi chose to turn pro. She became a headliner for Stars on Ice and established the Always Dream Foundation to help youngsters reach their goals. In 1998, she was inducted into the Hall of Fame.

MIDORI ITO

Winner of only one World Championship and an Olympic silver medal, Midori Ito was a trendsetter.

The greatest skater to come out of Japan, Ito was a jumping jack who needed many years to learn the grace and style of other skaters. Still, she was a top contender because she could hit any jump, including the difficult triple Axel, which few women had tried and none had landed when she completed it at the 1989 Worlds.

Ito was also the first woman to regularly do triple-triple jump combinations in competition.

Her success raised the popularity of figure skating in Asia.

NANCY KERRIGAN AND TONYA HARDING

Famous for their soap opera that turned figure skating into a nightly news subject in 1994, Nancy Kerrigan and Tonya Harding were talented skaters, too.

At a practice for the 1994 U.S. Championships in Detroit, Kerrigan was bashed on the knee by a man carrying an iron bar. Her injury forced her out of the event. An investigation later revealed that Tonya Harding's husband and several other men were behind the attack. They believed that by injuring Kerrigan, they would eliminate Harding's main competition for the 1994 Olympics in Lillehammer, Norway.

The United States Figure Skating Association (USFSA) wanted to suspend Harding from the Olympics, but it had no proof that she had been involved in the plot. Harding was allowed to compete. Kerrigan recovered so well that she won the short program at Lillehammer and skated sensationally in the free skate. Only the brilliance of the peppy Oksana Baiul of the Ukraine kept Kerrigan from winning.

Harding struggled with the media attention throughout the Games and was not a strong contender.

The Nancy Kerrigan/Tonya Harding saga was such a strange story that it lifted figure skating from the sports pages to the news pages. Figure skating's television ratings soared, both for the

Nancy Kerrigan leans back during a spin in the women's technical program at the 1994 winter Olympics, where she captured the silver medal.

traditional championships and the dozens of made-for-TV specials that the networks created.

When it became clear that she had known about the plot, Harding was suspended for life by the USFSA, but she was allowed to appear in professional events, over which the American federation, the ISU, and the IOC have no control. Soon after the 1994 Olympics, Kerrigan married and became a mother, but she continued to appear in ice shows and television specials.

4

THE ICE KINGS

While women's figure skating is known for its grace and beauty, mens' skating is famous for its speed and power. The men are expected to make the spins and jumps and steps look easy but still beyond the capability of the audience. Meet the Ice Kings:

DICK BUTTON

Most people involved in figure skating consider Dick Button to be the greatest of all men's skaters. Not only was Button the only American to win two Olympic gold medals (1948 and 1952), but he was also the first truly athletic free skater.

When Button was winning seven U.S. Championships and five straight World titles, free skating was not as important in the judging as it is today. In Button's era, the compulsories—required elements, including tracing figure eights on the ice—were worth 60 percent of the total score. They were later eliminated from competition, and the free skate became 66 percent of the overall score.

That, however, didn't prevent Button from being original. It seemed as if every year he came up with something new in his programs. A great leaper, Button was the first skater who actually jumped higher than the sideboards. Because of that jumping ability, he was the first competitor to do a double Axel, the most difficult of jumps

American figure skater Brian Boitano performs a jump during his routine at the 1994 U.S. Figure Skating Championships. One of the most artistic skaters of his time, Boitano brought romance, imagination, and showmanship to the ice.

Dick Button, four-time world champion and winner of a gold medal at the 1948 Olympics, leaps into the air during a practice session at Vienna, Austria's, ice stadium in 1951.

because it requires a front-facing takeoff and an extra half-turn in the air. He was the first to do a triple loop and double jumps in combination.

Button also invented the flying camel, a common move today for men and women in which the body flies parallel to the ice, with a leg remaining extended during the spin, after the skater lands on the other foot.

Button was so good that he forced changes in skating. In 1948, at age 18, he won the U.S., European, and World Championships and the Olympic gold medal. He was the first North American to win the Olympic men's figure skating title, at St. Moritz, Switzerland, and he is the only man to take those four championships in one year, because after 1948, Americans were no longer allowed to enter the European Championships.

The previous year, after Button finished second to Switzerland's Hans Gerschwiler at the Worlds (Gerschwiler was better in the compulsories, but Button was far superior in the free skate) ISU president Ulrich Salchow gave the second-place Button a trophy of his own.

In 1952, Button again won at the Olympics. He was the first figure skater to win the Sullivan Award for the best amateur athlete in America.

After his retirement from competition, Button skated professionally for a few years, while working toward a law degree. He also developed the television show *Superstars*, in which athletes competed in sports other than their own, and it was a big hit.

Button also created the first meaningful and successful professional skating events, and heading into the 21st century, his competitions remained the most important for non-Olympic-eligible skaters.

A member of the World Figure Skating Hall of Fame, Button has also been the voice of skating for four decades as the sport's best-known and most controversial commentator.

Before Button, most male skaters were technicians. He showed that they could be athletes too, and every top male skater since has combined the most difficult moves with the athletic ability, speed, and force that Button brought to the sport.

HAYES AND DAVID JENKINS

Hayes Jenkins won the Olympic gold medal in 1956, and his younger brother David won it in 1960. Hayes also won the U.S. and World Championships from 1953–56, and then his brother managed the same feat for the next three years. At the 1956 Olympics in Cortina, Italy, the Jenkins brothers joined with Ron Robertson to sweep the medals. Hayes Jenkins later married fellow Olympian Carol Heiss.

The sons of a skating judge, the Jenkins brothers were inducted into the Hall of Fame in 1976.

TOLLER CRANSTON

Although Toller Cranston wasn't the most successful competitive skater, he was a true artist.

The old-style judges didn't care much for his antics, but the fans loved them.

Cranston, a Canadian, was also a fine dancer, and he combined those skills with skating. He was more of a modern dancer than a classical skater, ignoring rounded lines and smooth movements, preferring to form unusual angles with his body. He also ignored the classical music used by nearly every skater, preferring to skate to jazz and songs from his time, the '60s and '70s.

He played a key role in changing the style of costumes from formal to modern, even outlandish. His colorful outfits often included sequins and rhinestones. Cranston's popularity soared as a professional, and he became a successful choreographer, coach, and costume designer.

DONALD JACKSON

The first of the great Canadian skaters who didn't play hockey, Jackson won the 1962 Worlds. A year earlier, an ill Jackson had canceled a reservation on an airplane that crashed, killing the entire U.S. figure skating team on its way to the World Championships.

Jackson put on the most memorable free skate the sport had seen at the '62 Worlds, hitting 22 jumps, including the first triple Lutz ever landed in competition, to win the title.

Jackson entered the Hall of Fame in 1977.

JOHN CURRY

John Curry, the 1976 Olympic champion, was the first great singles skater England produced. He also had a major influence on men's skating with the way he transferred ballet to the ice.

Throughout his career as a skater, Curry also studied and performed as a dancer. Not until the mid-1970s were his balletic moves accepted by the judges. By then, he had moved to the United States to work with coach Carlo Fassi.

In 1976, Curry gave in to the judges and changed his style a bit. He did more technical jumps, eliminating much of his expressiveness and drama. That year, Curry swept the European and World Championships and won the Olympic gold medal.

He then turned professional and formed a show in which he was able to combine ballet and skating with no concerns about judging. Curry, inducted into the Hall of Fame in 1991, died of AIDS in 1994.

ROBIN COUSINS

What John Curry began, countryman Robin Cousins took a few steps—and leaps and spins—further.

Cousins, the 1980 Olympic champion, overcame a weakness in the compulsories to win at Lake Placid, New York. He never won the Worlds because of that weakness, but in the biggest competition of his life, Cousins was superb.

Best known for his smooth elegance, he was often called the "Gene Kelly of the ice." Movie star Kelly was an athletic dancer; Cousins was an athletic dancer on ice. His remarkable footwork, often leading into difficult jumps or spins, was as original as anything the sport had ever seen.

Cousins later became a famous choreographer, designing routines for other skaters and

Scott Hamilton, shown during the free skating finals at the 1984 Olympics in Sarajevo, Yugoslavia, was the first American in 24 years to win an Olympic gold medal in figure skating.

for shows. He even appeared on stage in productions of *Cats* and *The Rocky Horror Picture Show.*

SCOTT HAMILTON

Scott Hamilton overcame a severe childhood illness to become a gold medalist and one of the most popular figure skaters ever. An intestinal disorder that stunted his growth and often forced him into hospitals plagued his early years. He needed a special diet and often used tubes to feed himself. Several doctors told Scott's adopted parents—he never knew his real parents—that he might die.

But Hamilton fought through the pain and embarrassment, and during a trip to Boston, a doctor told his family he simply needed a different diet and exercise. The exercise became figure skating.

Scott began to grow. He also took to the ice so naturally that by the time he was 18, Hamilton was a rising force in American figure skating. Like John Curry, Hamilton joined forces with coach Carlo Fassi. He almost quit skating when his mother died in 1978; then, despite a split with his coach, he persevered and made the 1980 Olympic team.

Hamilton was selected as the flag-bearer for the United States in the opening ceremonies at Lake Placid, and he finished fifth. From there, Hamilton skyrocketed to the top of the sport, winning the next four U.S. and World Championships, then taking the 1984 Olympics at Sarajevo, Yugoslavia.

But he was hardly through as an important figure in the sport. Hamilton, whose ability to spin like a top seemed to break the laws of nature, formed the Stars on Ice professional tour that became one of the two most popular ice shows in the world. He has also been a commentator for CBS.

In 1997, Hamilton was diagnosed with testicular cancer. Less than a year later, he was back on the ice, bringing his special brand of entertainment to fans everywhere.

BRIAN BOITANO AND BRIAN ORSER

The Battle of the Brians was the biggest story in men's figure skating for the years 1985–88. It was capped by a magnificent showing by the two Brians at the Calgary Olympics in 1988.

American Brian Boitano won four straight U.S. Championships heading to the Olympics and also took the '86 world title. Canadian Brian Orser owned the Canadian crown, winning it eight times, and was the 1987 world champion.

Good friends, Brian Boitano and Brian Orser still managed to keep the rivalry burning hot at the '88 Olympics. Boitano's routines were spotless, and when Orser cut short a jump, it was enough for the American's powerful skating to win out over the Canadian's precision. But both left lasting marks in the skating world with their dignity under pressure.

Among Boitano's gifts to skating was the "Tano," a unique triple Lutz jump in which he held a hand above his head. Boitano also produced and appeared in many television specials, opening new avenues for fans to see the best in figure skating.

Brian Orser skates in shows and does television specials in Canada, where he is also a figure skating commentator.

VICTOR PETRENKO

The Soviet Union dominated pairs and ice dancing in the 1970s, '80s and '90s. But the country's biggest breakthrough in singles didn't come until after the Soviet Union was broken up in the early 1990s.

Victor Petrenko, from the Ukraine, was the first Olympic gold medalist from a former Soviet republic. At the 1992 summer Olympics in Albertville, France, he was considered an outsider behind the Canadians and Petr Barna of Czechoslovakia.

But Petrenko, who won the bronze behind the two Brians in Calgary, put everything together at the 1992 Games, combining dramatic flair with sharp jumps and spins to capture the gold.

He quickly turned professional, moved to the United States, and became a megastar in touring shows. Nobody did a better Michael Jackson imitation than Petrenko, who provided funds and guidance to his countrywoman Oksana Baiul, helping her capture the 1994 Olympic gold.

KURT BROWNING AND ELVIS STOJKO

Although neither Canadian star won an Olympic title, they pretty much owned the World Championships in the late 1980s and the 1990s. Kurt Browning won Worlds in 1989, '90, '91, and '93. Elvis Stojko took them in 1994, '95, and '97.

Browning, like Hamilton before him, was a master showman, as well as a great jumper. In 1988 Browning became the first skater to land a quadruple (four-revolutions) jump in competition. Eventually, Browning became an actor on the ice. He would portray characters in many of his routines, from movie heroes to clowns.

As a professional, Browning further developed his character portrayals. By the late 1990s, he was the most popular male on tour.

While Browning broke new ground with his quadruple jump, it was Stojko who perfected it. He often did it in combination, including an incredible quad-triple combo that practically defied the laws of gravity.

Stojko favored martial arts themes in his skating, something it took the judges a while to accept. Like Orser, Stojko won two Olympic silver medals, capturing the second one in Nagano, Japan, in 1998, despite a torn groin muscle.

5

TWO FOR THE SHOW

If you think learning to do all of those difficult moves on skates—the jumps and spins and spirals—is unimaginably challenging, just think how tough it must be with a partner. In pairs skating and ice dancing, both skaters, one man and one woman, must be in unison. They mirror each other's moves. Add in the lifts and throws in pairs competition, and the need to be almost exactly in step with the music for ice dancing, and these disciplines become even more difficult to master. Not only do the partners' moves need to match, so do their moods.

Pairs skating didn't become part of the World Championships and Olympics until 1908, mainly because so few women were allowed to compete in figure skating in the early 1900s.

Ice dancing was first held at the Worlds in 1952, but it took until 1976 for it to become an Olympic sport.

Below is a look at the greatest pairs in history, followed by an examination of the best ice dancers.

Ekaterina Gordeeva and Sergei Grinkov, or "G & G," as they were known, took the gold medal for pairs figure skating at the 1994 European Figure Skating Championships held in Copenhagen, Denmark.

PAIRS SKATERS

ANDREE JULY AND PIERRE BRUNET

Both great singles skaters, this French husband and wife duo won Olympic gold medals in 1928 and 1932 and also captured three world titles.

They went on to become successful coaches in both singles and pairs.

July and Brunet used jumps and spins they borrowed from their singles careers, which earned them criticism from the sport's officials, who believed pairs skating should not be so athletic. But they were so good and so different that judges and fans alike accepted their daring style.

The Brunets were inducted into the Hall of Fame in 1976.

LUDMILLA AND OLEG PROTOPOPOV

The first of the great Russian pairs—and there have been hundreds who followed—the Protopopovs didn't begin skating until they were 15, very late for serious competitors. At first, they were not encouraged by sports officials in the Soviet Union, but they didn't back down and quickly earned success in the 1960s.

Known for their elegance and ability to mesh perfectly on every move, the Protopopovs

Oleg Protopopov dips his partner, Ludmilla, during the pairs figure skating competition at the 1964 Olympics in Innsbruck, Austria, where the Russian couple took the gold medal.

skated more slowly than other couples. But they were so graceful, powerful, and artistic that the more athletic pairs couldn't match them.

Gold medalists at the 1964 and 1968 Olympics, they also won four straight World Championships. Other pairs have tried to copy their style, but few have come close.

RODNINA AND ULANOV, RODNINA AND ZAITSEV

Irina Rodnina is considered the best of all pairs skaters because she became a champion with two partners. The Russian star won four Worlds and an Olympic gold medal with Alexei Ulanov. Then she won six Worlds and two more gold medals with Alexander Zaitsev.

Speed and energy were the trademarks of Rodnina and Ulanov, who formed a team in the 1960s while the Protopopovs were dominating pairs skating. They skated to louder, more powerful music. Their lifts and jumps were fast and athletic. They were as different from their countrymen as anyone possibly could be. They also were so good that Rodnina and Ulanov soared to the top of skating at their first Worlds in 1969. For the next decade, Rodnina would be the only woman to win gold at the Worlds.

In 1972, Ulanov fell in love with a pairs skater named Ludmila Smirnova, who became his partner. Rodnina tested more than 100 skaters before choosing Zaitsev as her new partner.

Usually, it takes years for a partnership to work in pairs skating. For Rodnina and Zaitsev, it took weeks. Zaitsev, more than a foot taller than Rodnina, seemed to lift her to the sky. On their throws, he seemed to send her halfway across the rink. Each time, Rodnina would land softly, perfectly.

She and Zaitsev married in 1975, in the middle of their run as the top duo in the sport. They retired in 1980 and eventually divorced.

Rodnina entered the Hall of Fame in 1989.

EKATERINA GORDEEVA AND SERGEI GRINKOV

Ekaterina Gordeeva was only 14 years old when she and Sergei Grinkov burst upon the world skating scene. By 1988, when she was 16, they owned two world titles and an Olympic gold medal.

After turning professional and joining the Stars on Ice tour, Gordeeva and Grinkov took advantage of a rule allowing pros a one-time return to the Olympics. In 1994, at the Lillehammer Games, their flowing beauty and precision earned them another gold medal.

Grinkov was 15 when he and Gordeeva, then 11, were matched by the Central Red Army Club in Moscow. Neither could jump well enough to be singles skaters, so they turned to pairs and turned the skating world upside-down.

Much of their style was based on ballet moves. But their lifts and throws were powerful, and they were perfectly in tune with the classical music they favored. Even against stronger, more mature competition at the 1988 and 1994 Olympics, "G & G," as they became known, won.

They were married in 1991. While rehearsing for a Stars on Ice show in Lake Placid, New York, on November 20, 1995, Grinkov collapsed on the ice and died of a heart attack.

The skating world mourned. Gordeeva wrote a book and hosted a skating tribute dedicated to her late husband.

Gordeeva became a singles skater in the late 1990s while still touring. She and her beloved Sergei were inducted into the Hall of Fame in 1995.

ICE DANCING

MARKHAM AND JONES, DENNY AND JONES

In the days before ice dancing became a permanent part of the figure skating scene, Courtney Jones was the dance leader.

Originally a pairs skater, he switched to ice dance in 1955, using the lessons he'd taken in ballroom dancing as a foundation. He had partnered with June Markham for only two months when they wound up second in the British Championships, an accomplishment followed by silver medals at the European and World Championships.

Jones, who had a job in the fashion industry, would head to the rink to practice after work, often staying on the ice until 2 A.M. While he and Markham were winning the 1957 and '58 Worlds, Jones was also developing two new ice dance patterns, the silver samba and the starlight waltz. Those dances are still used in competition today.

Markham soon tired of competition and retired to become a coach. Jones and his new partner, Doreen Denny, were just as successful, winning the next two World Championships. In 1962, Jones became a skating judge, and he also did some choreography and coaching. He was elected to the Hall of Fame in 1986.

JAYNE TORVILL AND CHRISTOPHER DEAN

Ask skating fans, judges, officials, and even other competitors to name the most memorable performance they've seen, and the answer probably would be one word: "Bolero."

When Jayne Torvill and Christopher Dean (T & D) came to the 1984 Sarajevo Games, they were already considered the greatest of all ice dance teams. Both from England, Torvill and Dean won four World Championships and changed their sport unlike anyone before or since.

T & D were willing to take chances to stretch the limits of their event. Dean invented moves and developed routines designed to make ice dancing an art form. Whether they were

British couple Jayne Torvill and Christopher Dean, who won a gold medal for ice dancing at the 1984 Olympics, dance Indian yoga at the 1985 International Pro Figure Skating Championship in Tokyo, Japan.

twisting themselves into pretzels or flowing together like swans, all eyes were fixed on them.

Ravel's "Bolero" is a swirling, teasing piece of music. T & D's program to it, which was practiced in secrecy for months, made its debut at the British Championships and immediately caused controversy. The complaints increased at the European Championships, where some of Torvill and Dean's rivals complained about what they considered illegal moves by the couple. Those European Championships were very tense, but when 11 of the 18 judges gave T & D perfect marks of 6.0, it was clear the sport was ready to be reinvented.

By the 1984 Olympics in Sarajevo, T & D were so well-known and popular that American television, which rarely showed ice dancing, scheduled the free dance for broadcast. What U.S. and world viewers saw was a masterpiece.

At Sarajevo, the Zetra Arena seemed completely silent, except for Ravel's music and the scratching of the blades on the ice, as Torvill and Dean set down their masterpiece. When they finished, the crowd exploded in cheers, which became deafening when the scores were posted. T & D earned nothing but 6.0s for artistry, something never before seen for any figure skating program.

Torvill and Dean went on to have a huge effect on ice dancing as professionals, trying new and unusual moves that soon became part of every couple's routines.

6 BEYOND COMPETITION

After their competitive careers are finished, most great skaters wind up in ice shows. Although there is an expanding professional circuit on which skaters can win contest medals, once the top men and women leave the Olympic-eligible ranks, they usually join a touring company.

For the last 12 years, the top two tours have been Stars on Ice, which was begun by Scott Hamilton in 1986, and the Champions on Ice troupe, which began in 1969.

Stars on Ice is more of a theatrical event, with each of the performers appearing on ice with one another, often in huge production numbers. As Hamilton wrote in the introduction to the book *Stars on Ice*:

"We have given the best in the world a place to take their skating far beyond what they were able to do as competitive athletes. A place where we aren't presenting just skating, but the best of what we are and hope to be."

Stars on Ice has been headlined by Hamilton, Kristi Yamaguchi, Rosalynn Sumners, Kurt Browning, Ekaterina Gordeeva and Sergei Grinkov, Jayne Torvill and Christopher Dean, and, recently, 1998 Olympic champions Tara Lipinski and Ilia Kulik. Through the years, such talented skaters as Katarina Witt, Paul Wylie, Brian Orser, Kitty and Peter Carruthers, Elena Bechke and Denis Petrov, Debi Thomas, and Dorothy Hamill have toured with the company.

Tara Lipinski, shown at the 1999 World Professional Championships, became a headliner for the Stars on Ice tour after turning professional. Created in 1986 by Scott Hamilton, the Stars on Ice tour showcases the talents and artistry of the world's top skaters.

After her upstart gold medal victory at the 1994 Olympics, Oksana Baiul turned pro and skated with the Champions on Ice tour.

While each skater or duo gets a chance to perform solo numbers, the highlight of a Stars on Ice presentation is the group number. One year, the troupe did an hilarious takeoff on Olympic figure skating. Another time, they did a serious tribute to the 1984 Sarajevo Games, remembering the best times of that city, which was torn by a long war soon after the Olympics.

Champions on Ice, which is owned by Tom Collins, features skaters performing the routines that made them famous. Collins was the first promoter to sign European skaters for an American tour.

"My first love is the tour," he says. "It's like having a child. I [was] with it from infancy to what it is today, and it was nurtured like a child. We saw it go from 15 cities to 90 cities with two tours. It's the highlight of my life and my career."

There are no large production numbers in Champions on Ice. It is an evening of pure skating, with the performers sometimes choosing a comical program, such as Victor Petrenko as Michael Jackson or Todd Eldredge as Charlie Chaplin.

Current headliners in Champions on Ice include Michelle Kwan, Alexei Yagudin, Victor Petrenko, Todd Eldredge, Oksana Baiul, and Nicole Bobek. Brian Boitano, the 1988 Olympic champion and one of skating's most popular figures, makes occasional appearances with the show.

The future of figure skating lies in three areas. The touring shows will always remain popular, because the top stars of the Olympics skate in them when they are not competing or have given up their eligibility. The professional events, backed by television, will present the best skaters of recent years who no longer desire to go through the grind of preparing for the Nationals, Worlds, or Olympics. And the Olympics will always be the focal point of competition, with the men doing more and more quadruple jumps and the women getting more and more artistic.

CHRONOLOGY

1772	Robert Jones of England writes the first book on ice skating.
1791	The first skating club is formed in Edinburgh, Scotland.
1850	The first skating club in the United States, the Philadelphia Skating Club and Humane Society, is formed.
1860	An estimated crowd of 100,000 skates on Christmas Day at the pond rink in New York's Central Park.
1863	The first organized U.S. Championships are held in Troy, New York.
1876	The Glacarium, the first rink with man-made ice, is opened in London.
1892	The International Skating Union is organized.
1896	The first men's World Championship is held in St. Petersburg, Russia.
1906	Women are allowed to compete at Worlds for the first time, in Davos, Switzerland.
1908	Figure skating becomes an Olympic event, although it is held at the summer Games in London; pairs competition is held for the first time at Worlds, although at a separate place from the singles event. The pairs are staged in St. Petersburg, while the men's and women's competitions are at Troppau, Czechoslovakia.
1921	The U.S. Figure Skating Association is created.
1924	The first winter Olympics are held in Chamonix, France.
1928	Sonja Henie wins the first of her three Olympic gold medals.
1948	The winter Olympics return after a 12-year absence caused by World War II; Dick Button and Barbara Ann Scott become the first North Americans to win gold medals for figure skating.
1961	An airplane crash kills the entire U.S. team as it travels to the World Championships in Czechoslovakia.
1968	ABC-TV televises the women's free skate in which Peggy Fleming wins the Olympic gold medal at Grenoble, France; after that broadcast, figure skating becomes the centerpiece of Olympic television; the value of the compulsory figures is reduced from 60 percent to 50 percent, with the free skate's worth moving from 40 percent to 50 percent.

CHRONOLOGY (CONTINUED)

1973   The technical, or short, program (20 percent) is added, with the compulsories and free skate then worth 40 percent each.

1976   The compulsories are reduced to 20 percent, with the technical program worth 30 percent and the free skate worth 50 percent.

1988   Skaters are allowed to earn money from the sport, although the money is placed in trust funds and can be used only for training and equipment.

1990   Compulsory figures are held for the last time at the World Championships. The free skate's value becomes 66.7 percent; the technical program, now called the short program, becomes worth 33.3 percent.

1994   Professionals with no more Olympic eligibility are allowed to return to the Olympics at Lillehammer; due in large part to the Nancy Kerrigan/Tonya Harding showdown, the 1994 Olympics at Lillehammer is the most-watched event in Olympic history.

1998   Tara Lipinski, at 15, becomes the youngest Olympic women's champion ever.

GLOSSARY

JUMPS

Axel – A combination of the waltz and loop jumps, with a forward takeoff. A simple axel is one revolution. The most difficult jump because of the extra half-turn, it is the only jump begun from a forward outside edge. It is landed on the back outside edge of the opposite foot.

Combination jump – Putting together two jumps, the second immediately after landing the first. Any two jumps can be done in combination.

Flip – A jump taken off from a back inside edge with the toe pick of the free leg dug into the ice, and landed on a back outside edge.

Loop – A jump in which the skater takes off from a back outside edge, turns once in the air and lands on the same back outside edge. As with most jumps, a double involves two turns; a triple involves three turns in the air.

Lutz – A toe jump similar to the flip, taken off from a backward outside edge with the toe pick of the free leg dug into the ice. The skater enters the jump skating in one direction and concludes the jump skating in the opposite direction. Usually performed in the corners of the rink.

Salchow – The skater takes off from the back inside edge of one foot and lands backward on the outside edge of the opposite foot from which the skater took off.

Toe Loop – A jump taken off from and landed on the same back outside edge, just as in a loop. But the skater kicks the toe pick at the front of the blade of the free leg into the ice upon takeoff, providing added power. Most skaters who attempt the four-revolution quadruple jump do a toe loop.

Toe Walley – Similar to a toe loop except the takeoff is from the inside edge.

Waltz – A simple jump involving a half-turn in the air, taken from a forward outside skate edge and landed on the back outside edge of the other foot.

SPINS

Camel Spin – A spin with the skater in an arabesque position, with the free leg at right angles to the leg on the ice.

Combination Spin – Putting together two or more spins, with the skater or skaters changing feet and positions while staying at the same speed through the whole spin

Flying Camel Spin – A jump spin ending in the camel-spin position.

Flying Sit Spin – A jump spin in which the skater leaps off the ice, assumes a sitting position at the peak of the jump, lands, and spins in a similar sitting position. Actually, the skater is squatting.

Layback Spin – A move in an upright spin position where the head and shoulders are dropped backward and the back arches.

Simple Spin – The rotation of the body in one place on the ice. Various spins include the back, fast or scratch, sit, and layback.

GLOSSARY (CONTINUED)

MOVEMENTS

Crossovers – A way of gaining speed and turning corners in which skaters cross one foot over the other. There are both forward and backward crossovers.

Gliding – The simple movement between stroking as the blades slide on the ice.

Spread Eagle – The skater leans either on the inside or outside edge as he or she glides in a circle, bending his or her body in the appropriate direction.

Stroking – The simple movement of stepping around the ice.

PAIR MOVEMENTS

Death Spiral – In perhaps the most dramatic move in skating, the man, acting as the center of a circle, holds tightly to the hand of his partner and pulls her around him. The woman, gliding on one foot, gets into a position almost parallel to the ice.

Lateral Twist – A move in which the man throws his partner overhead. She rotates once while in a lateral position to the ice and is caught.

Lifts – Any move in which the man lifts the woman off the ice. The man holds his partner above his head with one hand.

Throws – The man lifts the woman into the air and throws her away from him. She spins in the air and lands on one foot.

Twist – The man throws the woman into the air, she spins either twice or three times, and he catches her at the landing.

SCORING

Artistic Impression – The scoring category that judges the way the program was presented.

Factored Placement – The value for each event times the place the skater finished. For example, in singles and pairs, the short program is worth 33.3 percent of the total score. The free skate has a 66.7 percent value. Therefore, the short program has a .5 factor value, worth one-half of the free skate value, and the free skate has a 1.0 factor value. If a skater finishes third in the free skate, that is worth 3.0 factored placements (3 times 1.0). If a skater finishes third in the short program, that is worth 1.5 factored placements (3 times .5). The lowest factored placement total wins.

Ordinals – A score turned into a placement. If one skater is given a perfect 6.0, another a 5.9, and a third a 5.8, the skater with the 6.0 gets a first-place ordinal. The 5.9 earns a second-place ordinal, and the 5.8 gets a third-place ordinal. The skater with the most first-place ordinals wins.

When the total marks are equal for two or more skaters or pairs in free skating, the skater with the highest mark for artistry gets the ordinal.

Technical Merit – The scoring category that judges the difficulty of the skater's moves.

COMPETITION

Compulsories – Once the major part of competition, but no longer in use, they were the one-footed tracings of figure-eights with different parts of the blade.

Compulsory Dance – Each couple must do the same two dances to the same music, with scoring worth 10 percent of the total score for each dance.

Free Dance – Worth 50 percent of the total score, it has no required elements. The skaters choose the music, rhythm, and routine for their four-minute program.

Free Skate or Long Program – Worth 66.7 percent of the total score in singles and pairs, it has no required elements. The skaters choose the music and routine for their four and 1/2-minute program in men's and pairs; the women's free skate is four minutes long.

Original Dance – The type of music is decided beforehand, such as jazz, rock, waltz, or samba. The couples can choose their own music and perform an original routine to the required rhythm. It's worth 30 percent of the total score.

Technical or Short Program – A two-minute, 40-second routine in singles and pairs with eight required moves, set to music a skater chooses. All eight requirements, but no more, can be done. It is worth 33.3 percent of the total score.

MISCELLANEOUS TERMS

Eligible – Skaters who are allowed to compete in the Olympics, World Championships, Continental, and National Championships. They once were called amateurs.

IOC – The International Olympic Committee, which runs the winter and summer Olympics.

ISU – The International Skating Union, which runs or approves the sport's biggest events, such as the Olympics, World Championships, and National Championships in various countries.

Professionals – Skaters who are no longer eligible because they have become paid performers.

USFSA – The United States Figure Skating Association, which oversees the sport in the USA.

OLYMPIC CHAMPIONS

WOMEN

1908 – Madge Syers, Britain.
1920 – Magda Julin-Mauroy, Sweden.
1924 – Herma Plank-Szabo, Austria.
1928 – Sonja Henie, Norway.
1932 – Sonja Henie, Norway.
1936 – Sonja Henie, Norway.
1948 – Barbara Ann Scott, Canada.
1952 – Jeannette Altwegg, Britain.
1956 – Tenley Albright, United States.
1960 – Carol Heiss, United States.
1964 – Sjoukje Dijkstra, Holland.
1968 – Peggy Fleming, United States.
1972 – Beatrix Schuba, Austria.
1976 – Dorothy Hamill, United States.
1980 – Anett Poetzsch, East Germany.
1984 – Katarina Witt, East Germany.
1988 – Katarina Witt, East Germany.
1992 – Kristi Yamaguchi, United States.
1994 – Oksana Baiul, Ukraine.
1998 – Tara Lipinski, United States.

MEN

1908 – Ulrich Salchow, Sweden.
1920 – Gillis Grafstrom, Sweden.
1924 – Gillis Grafstrom, Sweden.
1928 – Gillis Grafstrom, Sweden.
1932 – Karl Schafer, Austria.
1936 – Karl Schafer, Austria.
1948 – Dick Button, United States.
1952 – Dick Button, United States.
1956 – Hayes Jenkins, United States.
1960 – David Jenkins, United States.
1964 – Manfred Schnelldorfer, West
    Germany.
1968 – Wolfgang Schwarz, Austria.
1972 – Ondrej Nepala, Czechoslovakia.
1976 – John Curry, Britain.
1980 – Robin Cousins, Britain.
1984 – Scott Hamilton, United States.
1988 – Brian Boitano, United States.
1992 – Victor Petrenko, Ukraine.
1994 – Alexei Urmanov, Russia.
1998 – Ilia Kulik, Russia.

PAIRS

1908 – Anna Hubler and Heinrich Burger, Germany.
1920 – Ludowika Jakobsson and Walter Jakobsson, Finland.
1924 – Helene Engelmann and Alfred Berger, Austria.
1928 – Andree July and Pierre Brunet, France.
1932 – Andree July and Pierre Brunet, France.
1936 – Maxie Herber and Ernst Baier, Germany.
1948 – Micheline Lannoy and Pierre Baugniet, Belgium.
1952 – Ria Falk and Paul Falk, West Germany.
1956 – Elisabeth Schwarz and Kurt Oppelt, Austria.
1960 – Barbara Wagner and Robert Paul, Canada.
1964 – Ludmila Belousova and Oleg Protopopov, Russia.
1968 – Ludmila Belousova Protopopov and Oleg Protopopov, Russia.
1972 – Irina Rodnina and Alexei Ulanov, Russia.
1976 – Irina Rodnina and Alexander Zaitsev, Russia.
1980 – Irina Rodnina and Alexander Zaitsev, Russia.
1984 – Elena Valova and Oleg Vasiliev, Russia.
1988 – Ekaterina Gordeeva and Sergei Grinkov, Russia.
1992 – Natalia Mishkutenok and Artur Dmitriev, Russia.
1994 – Ekaterina Gordeeva and Sergei Grinkov, Russia.
1998 – Oksana Kazakova and Artur Dmitriev, Russia.

ICE DANCING

1976 – Ludmila Pakhomova and Aleksandr Gorshkov, Soviet Union.
1980 – Natalia Linichuk and Gennadi Karponosov, Soviet Union.
1984 – Jayne Torvill and Christopher Dean, Britain.
1988 – Natalia Bestemianova and Andrei Bukin, Soviet Union.
1992 – Marina Klimova and Sergei Ponomarenko, United Team.
1994 – Pasha Grishuk and Evgeny Platov, Russia.
1998 – Pasha Grishuk and Evgeny Platov, Russia.

FURTHER READING

DuPont, Lonnie Hull. *Oksana Baiul*. Philadelphia: Chelsea House Publishers, 1999.

Edelson, Paula. *Nancy Kerrigan*. Philadelphia: Chelsea House Publishers, 1999.

Harper, Suzanne. *Boitano's Edge*. New York: Simon and Schuster, 1997.

Jones, Veda Boyd. *Nicole Bobek*. Philadelphia: Chelsea House Publishers, 1999.

——— . *Tara Lipinski*. Philadelphia: Chelsea House Publishers, 1999.

Kelly, Evelyn B. *Katarina Witt.* Philadelphia: Chelsea House Publishers, 1999.

Kwan, Michelle. *The Winning Attitude*. New York: Hyperion Books, 1999.

Lipinski, Tara. *Totally Tara*. New York: Universe, 1998.

Shea, Pegi Deitz. *Ekaternia Gordeeva.* Philadelphia: Chelsea House Publishers, 1999.

U.S. Figure Skating Association. *The Official Book of Figure Skating*. New York: Simon and Schuster, 1998.

Wellman, Sam. *Kristi Yamaguchi*. Philadelphia: Chelsea House Publishers, 1999.

——— . *Michelle Kwan*. Philadelphia: Chelsea House Publishers, 1998.

Wilner, Barry. *Stars on Ice*. Kansas City: Andrews McMeel, 1998.

Yamaguchi, Kristi. *Always Dream*. Dallas: Taylor Publishing, 1998.

INDEX

PICTURE CREDITS Associated Press/WWP: pp. 2, 6, 9, 10, 18, 20, 25, 30, 32, 34, 36, 40, 44, 50, 52, 54, 56; Corbis-Bettmann: pp. 28, 46; National Archives: p. 14; New York Public Library: p. 17.

BARRY WILNER has been a sportswriter for the Associated Press since 1975. He has covered a wide range of events, from the summer and winter Olympics to the Super Bowl, the World Cup, the U.S. Open, and the World and U.S. Championships in figure skating. He has written 14 books. Barry lives in Garnerville, New York, with his wife Helene, daughters Nicole, Jamie, and Tricia, and son Evan.